Corn Crazy

Written by Marilyn Woolley

Flying Start
to Literacy®

Contents

Introduction

Corn has been grown for thousands of years and has become one of the world's most important food crops. In fact, it is such an important source of food that corn is celebrated in corn festivals in many different countries.

Corn may seem like just another vegetable, but in fact, corn is used to make an incredible number of different things. You may know that people eat corn, but did you know that parts of the corn plant are also used to make peanut butter, toothpaste and even car fuel?

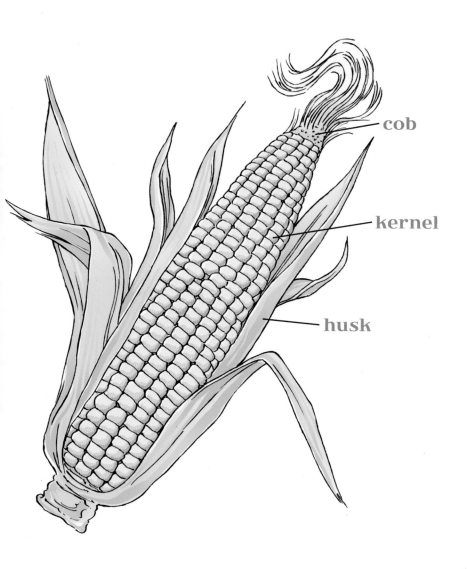

cob

kernel

husk

The whole corn plant, including the husk and the cob, is used in many different ways. Corn is used in more than 3000 supermarket products.

Chapter 1

Let's eat!

Corn is used to make a lot of different foods, including some very popular ones.

Crunchy corn flakes

Corn flakes are made from corn kernels. The kernels are roughly ground and then cooked with syrup, flavouring and salt. The corn flakes are then flattened by big machines and toasted.

Popping popcorn

Popcorn is also made from corn kernels. When corn is heated, it "pops" and puffs up. Each kernel of corn has a hard covering called a hull that is filled with starch. When it's heated, the starch expands and explodes in a pop. Popcorn often has salt or sugar added to it.

Corn crazy fact

Corn is also called maize. Over 150 million hectares of corn are planted across the world each year.

Tasty tortillas

This flat corn bread was first made in Mexico thousands of years ago. Today, it is still made the same way it was long ago in Mexico. Some tortillas are fried to make them crisp. They can also be made into corn chips by cutting the tortillas into triangular wedges and then deep-frying them. These chips can be eaten with dips or with melted cheese – we call this dish nachos.

Tempting tacos

Tacos are made when tortillas are folded or wrapped around food added as a filling. Tacos can be filled with beans, seafood, chicken, beef, cheese and salad vegetables.

Extreme enchiladas

Enchiladas are like tacos and have similar fillings, but they are usually covered in a chili-pepper or tomato sauce and baked in the oven.

Chapter 2

Corn-crazy world

Corn plants are grown all around the world, on every continent except Antarctica. Today, more corn is grown each year than any other grain, including wheat or rice.

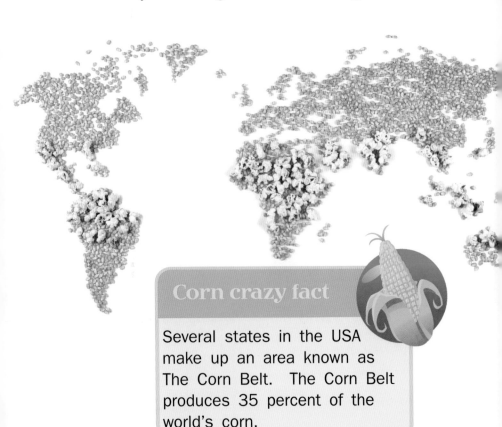

Corn crazy fact

Several states in the USA make up an area known as The Corn Belt. The Corn Belt produces 35 percent of the world's corn.

From cobs to make-up

Corn on the cob is many people's favourite food. But corn has many other uses.

Corn kernels are ground into fine white powder to make cornflour. Some people who cannot eat wheat use cornflour instead of wheat flour to make bread, cakes and muffins. It is also used in cooking to thicken soups and sauces.

Dry corn powder is used as a chemical in plastics and make-up. And dried corn cobs can be used for heating instead of wood.

From cornflour to car fuel

Cornflour is not just used in cooking. It is also used in paper products, shoe polish and to make glue. The plasterboard that is on the ceilings and walls of many houses is made using cornflour.

A type of fuel for cars can also be made from corn. In the future, corn could be used more and more to make fuel for cars, trucks and buses.

From syrup to toothpaste

Corn syrup is a thick, sweet liquid that is made from corn. Much of the food we buy at the supermarket contains corn syrup. It is used to sweeten food such as snack bars, peanut butter, cereals, salad dressings, lollies, cakes, muffins, soft drink, ice cream and popcorn. But did you know it is also used in toothpaste?

From corn husks to puppets

Each cob of corn is wrapped tightly in layers of leaves called a husk. Corn husks can be used to wrap fish for baking or grilling. Dried husks can be used to make puppets and dolls. And they can be used to get a fire started while camping.

From corn plants to animal feed

Animals such as cows and sheep eat the whole corn plant. The corn plants are harvested while they are still green. The whole plant is chopped up and stored in a silo. This feed is called silage.

Corn crazy fact

The kernels from a corn cob can be yellow, brown, white, red or blue.

Chapter 3
The fastest growing grain

Corn is one of the fastest growing food plants. In spring, farmers plant corn seeds in rows in the ground. The corn plants are fully grown in 80 to 120 days. Each tall, green stalk can produce two or three ears or cobs from its flowers.

The corn plant grows slowly until it reaches 60 centimetres, then it grows very fast – it can grow a new leaf every three days.

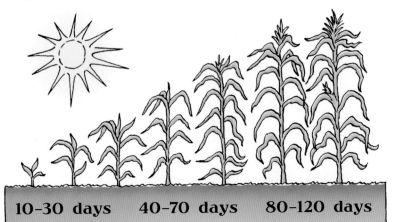

10–30 days   40–70 days   80–120 days

Corn needs a lot of sunshine to grow well. On hot summer nights a corn plant can grow five to seven centimetres taller. During autumn, people look to see when the silk in the husk changes to a dark brown colour. This means the corn is ready to be picked.

Corn crazy fact

Some types of corn plants can grow as tall as 7 metres. Corn cobs are different lengths too. They can be as long as 20 centimetres or as small as 2.5 centimetres.

Chapter 4
Corn through time

The earliest record we have of people eating corn is in South America. Archaeologists have excavated tools that contain traces of corn. The Aztec and Mayan peoples of Mexico developed corn from a type of grass.

This statue of a maize goddess is from the Aztec empire and is about 600 years old.

Archaeologists have also found paintings and carvings of corn on pottery, rocks, caves and sculptures underground in the places where these people lived.

Soon people in Peru and other parts of South America began to grow corn. They developed different types of corn. Corn spread into North America, where the Native Americans used it for food and for trading.

Today, people around the world grow different types of corn to suit their needs.

Corn goes global

About 500 years ago, the Spanish sailed to the Americas, where they ate corn for the first time. They took the corn plant back to Europe, where it spread into Africa, the Middle East and Asia.

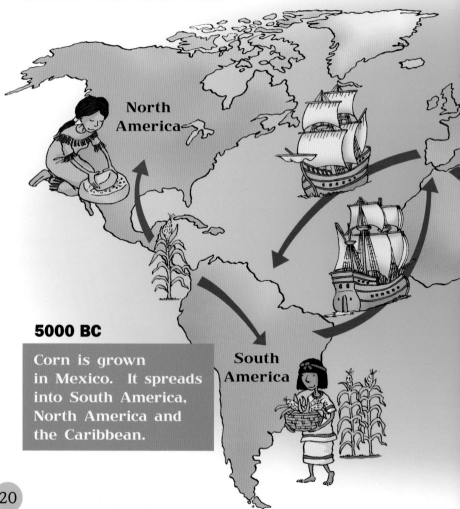

North America

South America

5000 BC

Corn is grown in Mexico. It spreads into South America, North America and the Caribbean.

1493

The Spanish sail to South America. They bring corn back to Europe.

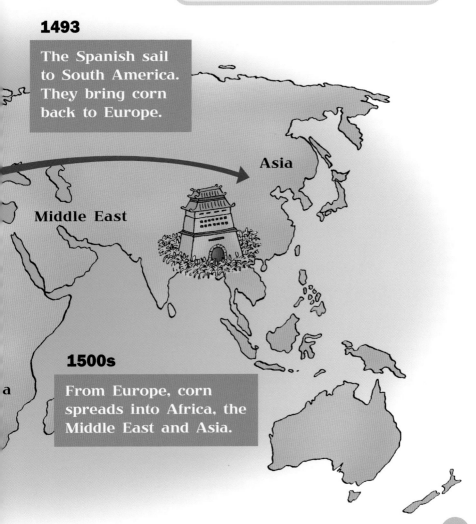

Asia

Middle East

1500s

From Europe, corn spreads into Africa, the Middle East and Asia.

a

Chapter 5
Celebrating corn

Corn has become such an important crop that people even have festivals to celebrate corn harvests. In parts of the USA where a lot of corn is grown, festivals have been held for many years. People come together to cook corn, dance, sell crafts made from corn and raise money to help people in their community. At some corn festivals, huge pots are filled with about 1100 litres of boiling water to cook more than 1000 cobs of corn every nine minutes.

The Mendota Sweet Corn Festival in the US state of Illinois lasts for four days. Over 60000 people eat enough corn at the festival to fill seven big trucks!

Thanksgiving

When people first came from parts of Europe to the USA, Native Americans showed them how to grow corn and how to prepare it in different ways. Corn became an important plant for European farmers as they settled in more and more parts of the USA.

Native Americans helped the first European settlers to farm corn.

These settlers are sharing a harvest meal with Native Americans.

The Native Americans continued to help the farmers grow healthy crops, and the farmers thanked them by preparing a large meal for them. This feast became known as Thanksgiving. Thanksgiving is still celebrated each year in the USA.

Corn crazy fact

Corn was eaten at the first Thanksgiving feast in 1621.

Corn glossary

cob   made up of about 800 kernels in 16 rows

ear   includes the cob, kernels, husk and silk.
Many ears grow on a corn plant.

husk   leaves that cover the cob of corn.
The husk protects the cob.

kernels   seeds of the corn plant.
They are the part of the plant you can eat.

silk   long thread that is attached to each kernel

stalk   stem of a corn plant

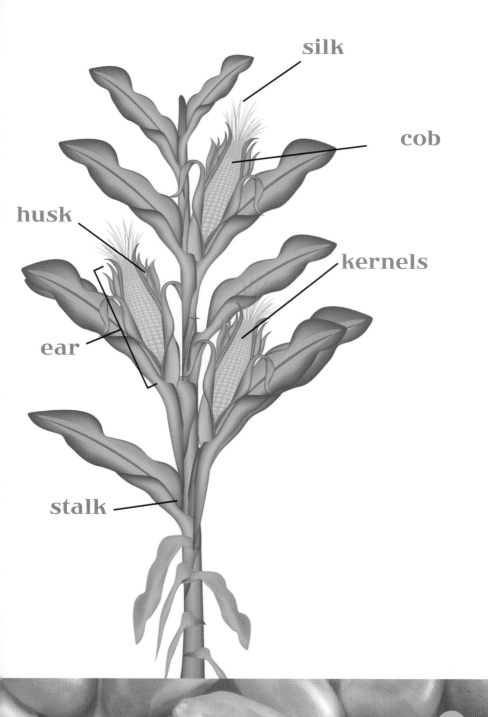

silk

cob

husk

kernels

ear

stalk

A note from the author

I first found out about corn when my parents grew it in our garden. We used it as food for our family and to feed the cows on our dairy farm.

Over time I have became aware of how people all over the world use different parts of the corn plant to make millions and millions of products. New uses of corn are being invented all the time.

I thought it would be interesting to do some more research on corn and write a book about how people have become corn crazy.